Billy
Loves Birds

happy yak

Inspiring | Educating | Creating | Entertaining

Brimming with creative inspiration, how-to projects, and useful information to enrich your everyday life, quarto.com is a favorite destination for those pursuing their interests and passions.

Text © 2022 Jess French
Illustrations © 2022 Duncan Beedie

Jess French has asserted her right to be identified as the author of this work. Duncan Beedie has asserted his right to be identified as the illustrator of this work.

Designer: Mike Henson
Commissioning Editor: Carly Madden
Editor: Victoria Garrard
Creative Director: Malena Stojić
Associate Publisher: Rhiannon Findlay

First published in 2022 by Happy Yak, an imprint of The Quarto Group.
100 Cummings Center, Suite 265D Beverly, MA 01915, USA.
T (978) 282-9590 F (978) 283-2742
www.quarto.com

A CIP record for this book is available from the Library of Congress.

ISBN 978 0 7112 6558 5

Manufactured in Guangdong, China TT012022

9 8 7 6 5 4 3 2 1

FSC
www.fsc.org
MIX
Paper from responsible sources
FSC® C016973

STAY SAFE!

Bird-watching is a lot of fun if you follow these guidelines:

- Take a grown-up with you to keep you safe.

- Always treat birds kindly and take care of the places that they live in.

- Don't drop litter and stay on the paths.

- Never touch bird eggs (it's ok to pick up pieces of shell if they are on the ground).

- Never climb up to a bird's nest.

- If you find a chick on the ground, ask a grown-up what to do.

- When you get home, wash your hands with soap and water, especially before eating.

DUNCAN BEEDIE

Billy Loves Birds

I'm Billy's friend Terry. I'm never far away from Billy so keep an eye out for me!

happy yak

HELLO, I'M BILLY.
I LOVE BIRDS. Wherever I go, I'm always on the lookout for new feathered friends. I'm going to forest school today— I always see lots of birds there. I can't wait!

I'd better get dressed.

If only I could change my feathers like that!

No time to waste—I'm hoping to see something very exciting today!

Now I need to brush my teeth.

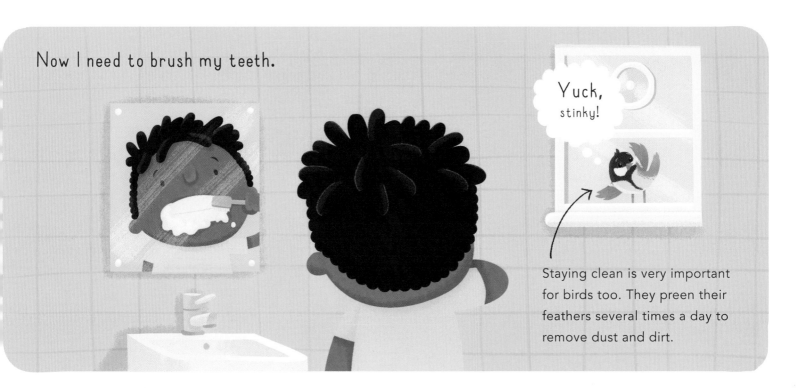

Yuck,
stinky!

Staying clean is very important
for birds too. They preen their
feathers several times a day to
remove dust and dirt.

Time for breakfast!

Now I'm going to see what some
of my bird friends are up to.

This nest belongs to an **ostrich**.
The eggs are enormous!

Ostriches are the heaviest
birds in the world. They
can't fly so they make
their nests on the ground.

This video is coming live from a nest camera
in Africa. The camera is placed near the nest,
so it's easy to see what's happening inside
without disturbing the bird or its chicks.

Look! One of the eggs is hatching. There's a little hole!
I can hear the chick's beak pecking on the inside of the shell.

PIP! PIP!

Hello, baby ostrich!

I love nest cameras! This bird's nest is at my forest school. I watched these chicks hatch so I can't wait to visit them today.

Ooh look, they are having their breakfast. Caterpillars!

Baby chicks spend the first few weeks of their lives eating and growing in the safety of the nest.

Just one thing left to do before school—I need to fill up the bird feeders.

Mmmm! Where shall I start?

Bird feeders can be filled with all sorts of tasty treats.

Mealworms

Mixed seeds

Sunflower seeds

Fat balls

Full of calories, fat balls are perfect for helping birds to keep warm in the cold winter months.

Oops, I spilled some! Never mind, greedy blackbirds and other ground feeders will quickly gobble up the tasty snacks.

You can make bird feeders out of almost anything. Make sure to keep them clean, so that they will not make the birds sick.

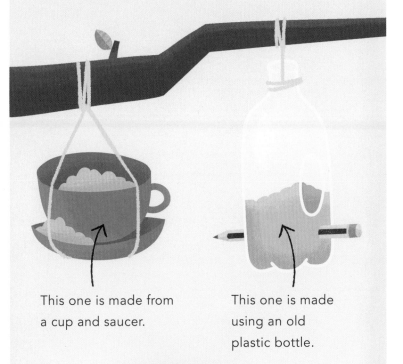

This one is made from a cup and saucer.

This one is made using an old plastic bottle.

I love to make new bird feeders. This one, built using LEGO® bricks, is my favorite.

I leave water out for the birds too. "Hello! Are you thirsty?"

Just like us, birds need to drink to stay healthy.

Now it's time to leave for forest school. Hmmm, now where is my bag?

Ah, here it is!
It has everything I need
for a day exploring.

BOOTS—to keep my
feet cozy and dry.

BACKPACK
—to store all my
equipment in.

I prefer to
travel light.

10

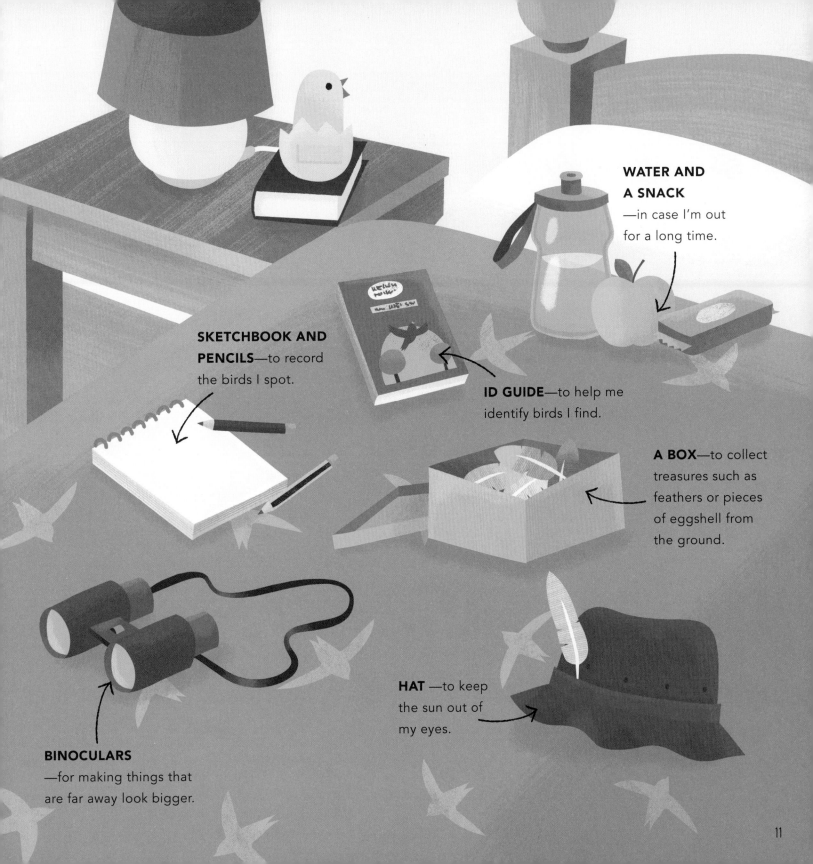

WATER AND A SNACK—in case I'm out for a long time.

SKETCHBOOK AND PENCILS—to record the birds I spot.

ID GUIDE—to help me identify birds I find.

A BOX—to collect treasures such as feathers or pieces of eggshell from the ground.

BINOCULARS—for making things that are far away look bigger.

HAT—to keep the sun out of my eyes.

Off we go!

These birds are really enjoying the sunflower seeds.

"Yay—the hanging feeder is busy!"

These birds love fat balls! They often arrive in large, noisy groups—but you have to be quick to see them, they don't hang around for long.

"Hello fluff-balls! Are you hungry?"

As well as drinking, birds use water to wash their feathers and stay cool.

"Wow, you are really enjoying your bath today, birds! Watch out—you're splashing me!"

This **house martin** has picked up some mud in its beak. It will use the mud to build its nest. It can take up to 10 days to build, but once it is made, the nest can be reused for many years to come.

"Each species of bird has its own special way of nest-building. Let's check out some other incredible nests..."

BILLY'S TOP BIRD NESTS

A nest is a shelter where a bird lays its eggs.

1. **Baya weaver** nests dangle from trees like fruit. They are made of woven grass and can be as big as a soccer ball.

3. Busy **bee-eaters** burrow into sandy riverbanks or cliffs to make their nests.

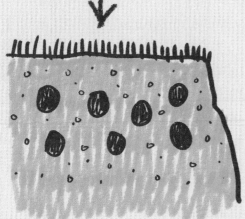

2. Plucky **Gila woodpeckers** nest inside prickly cactuses in the desert!

4. **African jacanas** build incredible nests that float on water.

5. **Eagles** build large nests, called eyries, high in trees or on top of cliffs.

6. **Common tailorbirds** stitch leaves together to create their nests.

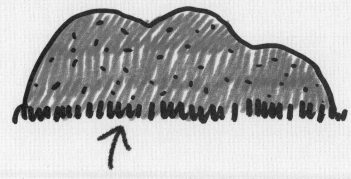

7. **Brush turkeys** make their nests from soil and dead leaves. The mounds can be as big as a car!

8. Sociable **weavers** mainly live in Asia and Africa. They create enormous nests where more than a hundred birds can lay their eggs.

9. **House martins** build their mud nests on cliff faces, the outside of buildings, or under the eaves of roofs.

I pass this pond every day on my way to forest school. I love to see what all the birds are doing—you can learn so much just by watching.

Lakes and ponds are a great place to spot birds. How many different types can you see here?

Yay! Snack time!

Ducks can sleep with one eye open to watch out for danger.

The **mallards** are preening! They use their beaks to spread a special waxy layer over their wings. This makes their feathers waterproof and keeps them warm and dry.

Male ducks are called **drakes**. They are often very brightly colored.

Swans use their long necks to reach down and grab underwater plants.

Many ducks feed by sticking their heads under the water — this is called "dabbling."

Herons stand very still in the water, searching for fish or frogs to catch.

I've arrived at forest school and have found my friend Bella. She loves bugs and is always digging around in the dirt searching for creepy-crawly friends.

"Hi Billy! I'm worm charming. If you stamp on the ground, worms think it's raining and come up to the surface. Do you want to try?"

STAMP!

STAMP!

STAMP!

SOUNDS LIKE THUNDER!

Some birds stamp their feet on the ground to attract worms like this too. Once the worms reach the surface they gobble them up!

18

"Look at the seagull! He's picked up one of the worms. He's probably taking it to feed his babies. Let's follow him and see where he goes!"

Growing chicks are very hungry. Their parents work hard all day to keep them fed.

"Try not to be sad, Bella. It's all part of the circle of life."

"Look, he's flying away!"

Seagulls make their nests at the seaside, on sand dunes, cliffs, and even on rooftops!

TOO MUCH NOISE!

PECK

PECK

PECK

PECK

"Hold on, can you hear that sound? Something is drumming on the tree."

"I think it's a woodpecker!"

Woodpeckers drum on hollow trees to let other woodpeckers know where they are, and to claim an area of land as their own— this is called their territory.

"Come on, Bella, let's be woodpeckers!"

Can you peck like a woodpecker too?

"Wow, all the noise has attracted the female woodpecker!

Look at her powerful beak! I'm going to sketch her."

Woodpeckers also use their beaks to make holes in bark and pluck insects from the ground. They have long tongues to lap up insects.

BILLY'S 10 BEST BIRD BEAKS

Bird beaks are sometimes called bills.

1. The brightly colored beaks of **puffins** have earned them the nickname "clowns of the sea."

2. **Pelicans** use their huge beaks to catch fish.

3. The sensitive beaks of **spoonbills** help them find insects and fish to eat.

4. **Hornbills** have huge growths, called casques, on top of their beaks.

5. **Crossbills** have beaks that are perfect for removing the seeds from inside pine cones.

6. **Hummingbirds** use their sword-like beaks for reaching nectar deep inside flowers.

7. **Toucans** have huge, colorful beaks.

8. **Kiwis** are the only birds that have their nostrils at the end of their beaks! Other birds have nostrils close to their faces.

9. **Flamingos** hold their heads upside down in the water to use their beaks as filters.

10. **Hawks** use their hooked beaks for eating meat.

Time to go. This path through the woods will take me to the bird's nest, but it's full of crunchy twigs that might scare the birds away.

I wonder if walking on my tiptoes will be quieter?

CRUNCH!

CRUNCH!

Or even better, crawling on all fours!

There's lots to see down here on the ground. Here are some new plants pushing up through the soil—sparrows love to eat those.

Oh, some springy moss—finches would love to line their nests with that.

But what's this? An empty eggshell! It's small and pale blue. I wonder where it came from.

Never get too close to bird's nests—you could hurt the babies inside, or frighten away the parents.

Oh, look—here is a nest of eggs! I'll check in my book which bird they belong to.

These look like the right eggs. It must be a robin nest, but one of the eggs in the nest is speckled, not blue. I wonder why...

Robin
(*Turdus migratorius*)

Oh, what a lovely sound! A cowbird must be somewhere nearby. Maybe the extra egg belongs to her?

TWEET! TWEET!

I've never seen a cowbird chick before. I will come back in a few days, to see if any of the eggs have hatched. In the meantime, I'll check the eggs in my book...

Never take eggs out of a nest. Only collect broken eggshells that you find on the ground.

Robin parents often spot the cowbird eggs and throw them out, but not always. When the cowbird egg hatches, the robin parents look after the cowbird chick as well as their own

Extraordinary Eggs

All birds have their babies by laying eggs.

Cuckoos don't build their own nests. Instead, they lay their eggs in the nests of other birds.

Hummingbird eggs are tiny. Some of them are no bigger than a baked bean!

Penguins keep their eggs warm by holding them on their feet, where they press against their warm bellies.

Ostriches lay the biggest eggs of all birds; each ostrich egg is as big as 27 chicken eggs.

 x 27

27

There's my friend Ava. She loves learning about animals. I wonder what she's doing...

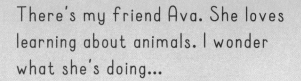

"Hi, Billy. Look, I've found some animal tracks!

That's strange, the mouse footprints stop here. I wonder why."

Mouse tracks

Ducks have three large toes pointing forward. These toes have flaps of webbed skin between them to help the ducks swim.

Herons have large feet, with four big toes and no webbed skin between them.

"Maybe this is a clue about the mouse tracks. Do you know what it is?"

"Oh ! That's an owl pellet. Maybe the mouse was eaten by an owl."

Owls feed on small animals like mice and shrews, but there are some bits of those animals that they can't digest. Those bits are released in a pellet instead.

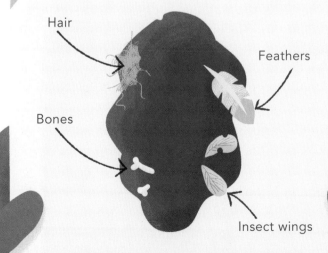

What's inside an owl pellet?

Hair

Feathers

Bones

Insect wings

"Wow! Billy, did you see that bird? It was like blue lightning flashing into the water! Look, it's over on that perch now."

SPLASH!

"I'll get my binoculars to see it more clearly!"

"It's a ringed kingfisher! Its wings are electric blue and its belly is bright orange. Ooh, it has a fish in its beak!"

"Can I see, please?"

"The fish is a stickleback. I can see the spines on its back. What a beautiful bird. I would love to have feathers like that."

Kingfishers are fantastic at fishing. A kingfisher spends most of its time waiting near the edge of a river, but when a fish swims close to the surface it dives under the water to snatch the fish for its lunch.

Aren't kingfisher feathers incredible? I collect feathers, would you like to see?

"Look at these!"

All birds have feathers. They can be thick, thin, long, short, bright or dull. They are very important for keeping birds warm and dry, and most importantly, birds need their feathers to fly!

Wing feathers
Big and strong. They give birds shape and help them to steer when they are flying.

"This feather is from a screech owl...

Down feathers
Fluffy and soft. They keep birds toasty and warm.

"This feather is from a goose."

Tail feathers
Some birds use their tail feathers in flight, but others use them to show off!

...and this is from a pheasant."

Fabulous feathers

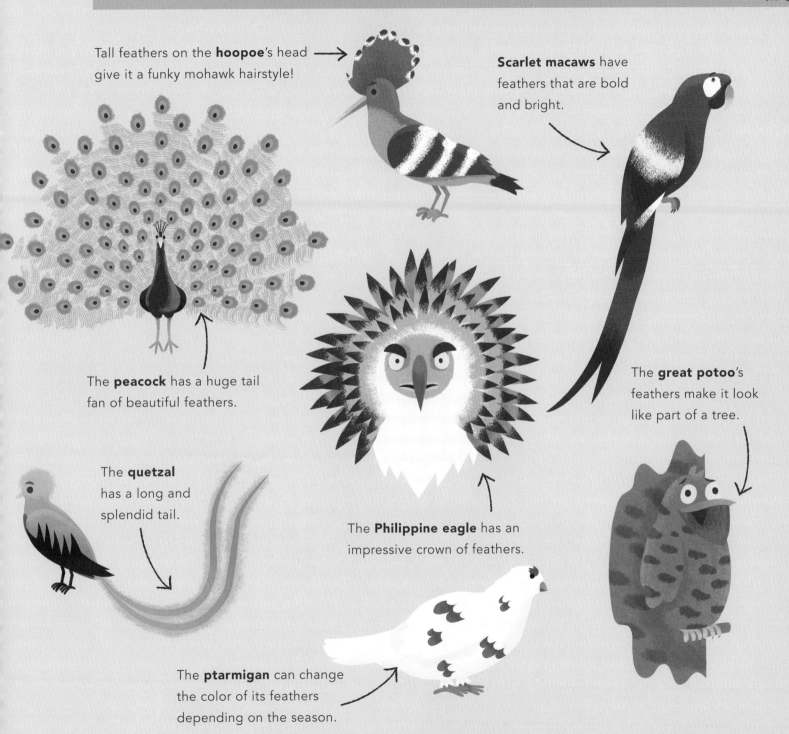

Tall feathers on the **hoopoe**'s head give it a funky mohawk hairstyle!

Scarlet macaws have feathers that are bold and bright.

The **peacock** has a huge tail fan of beautiful feathers.

The **great potoo**'s feathers make it look like part of a tree.

The **quetzal** has a long and splendid tail.

The **Philippine eagle** has an impressive crown of feathers.

The **ptarmigan** can change the color of its feathers depending on the season.

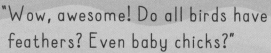
"Wow, awesome! Do all birds have feathers? Even baby chicks?"

"Sometimes chicks do have feathers, but some kinds of chicks are born without any.

I've been watching some chicks grow. They have their flight feathers now, so they are ready to make their first flights. I think they might do it today."

For me? Thanks!

When a bird is born without feathers, it takes a while for them to grow. The downy feathers are replaced with scruffy grown-up ones and their wing muscles grow big and strong.

"I better go. I don't want to miss anything."

Nearly there! The nest box is just over there.

TWEET! TWEET!

Wait. What was that? It sounds a little bit like somebody whistling a tune. There must be a bird singing somewhere nearby.

There it is! What a beautiful sound it's making.

Some kinds of birds are called songbirds. Songbirds have special voice boxes, which allow them to sing beautiful songs. Each bird has its own special tune, and, if you listen to birds enough, you can start to identify them by the sound of their songs.

Birds make all kinds of different sounds. Have a try...

Can you trumpet like a **crane**?
HOOT HOOT

Can you caw like a **crow**?
CAW CAW

Can you hoot like **tawny owls**?
TWIT TWOO TWIT TWOO

Can you call like a **cuckoo**?
CUCK-OO CUCK-OO

Can you whistle like a **blackbird**?
TWEET TWEET TWEET

Can you warble like a **chiffchaff**?
CHIFF CHAFF CHIFF CHAFF

Can you laugh like a **kookaburra**?
HA HA HA HA HA

Can you coo like a **turtledove**?
COO COO COO

Can you copy like a **parrot**?
PIECES OF EIGHT

GOOD JOB!

Sometimes birds sing to attract other birds, sometimes they call to warn other birds to stay away and sometimes their calls can be a warning that there is danger nearby.

"Hi, Pedro! I'm practicing my bird calls. What are you doing?"

"I've been picking up litter!"

Humans create lots of trash. If our litter gets into the environment, it can cause a lot of damage.

"Wow, you've found so much."

"I know, there's plastic everywhere. That's why I try not to use plastic things."

Animals sometimes eat small pieces of plastic by mistake, thinking they are food. It can make them really sick.

"I hope the chicks I'm watching won't eat any plastic. I want them to be strong and healthy."

"I can help you clear up the trash near their nest, if you like? Here, take these. We can pick up any litter we see as we go."

"Wow, what was that?"

"It looks like a **peregrine falcon**! Look, it's chasing that pigeon."

WHOOSH!

"It's so fast!"

"Faster than any other animal on the planet! When it "stoops" it folds its wings up like this...

Hey!
Watch out Billy!

...then shoots through the air."

"Birds are perfectly designed to zoom through the air. Some of them can fly extremely fast, others fly very high or very far. Today, my chicks are going to learn to fly for the first time. I can't wait!"

Peregrine falcons have excellent eyesight to spot their prey. It is much better than ours—we need to use binoculars to see things that are far away clearly.

A peregrine can reach speeds of over 200 miles per hour—that's faster than a race car!

Flight

Birds have air inside their bones to make them less heavy.
Their strong, light feathers help them steer.

Arctic terns can fly up to 50,000 miles each year. That's equivalent to circling Earth—twice!

Hummingbirds can fly forward and backward, and can dart and dive.

Bar-headed geese fly as high as airplanes.

Some birds move to warmer countries during the winter months. This is called migration.

Huge **albatrosses** use their enormous wings to soar over the oceans.

Migrating birds often fly in a V-shape to save energy.

"Look, there's the nest box! Mr. Patel helped me put it there."

"It's so high up! How will the chicks know what to do?"

Many birds like to make their nests in holes in trees, but sometimes they will use nest boxes made by humans.

"The chicks just have to be brave. If we are very quiet we might see them take their first flight."

Nests that are high up keep birds safe from other animals and give them plenty of space to fly in and out.

Like humans learning to walk, flying is a skill that baby birds have to learn.

"For the last few days, the chicks have been flapping and stretching their wings in preparation for leaving the nest."

When the chicks leave the nest it is a big and scary moment! They are a long way up and they have never flown before.

"Look, the mommy bird has brought her chicks a snack. Come on, little chicks!'

"It's hard to believe that just three weeks ago they were hatching from their eggs!"

The mom and dad are calling. They are encouraging the chick to leave the nest.

LEAVING THE NEST

BRANCHING
Before they can fly, **tawny owl** chicks hop and clamber through the trees. This is called branching.

LEARNING TO SWIM
Ducklings can learn to swim hours after hatching, but it can take them months to learn to fly.

LEAP OF FAITH
Barnacle goslings leap from their cliff-top nests, which can be as high as twenty giraffes above the ground.

"THEY DID IT! Well done, little chicks. Time to head off and explore the big wide world now."

FLAP

FLAP

FLAP

YAY!

Now that they have left the safety of the nest, the young birds must start to find their own food.

"That was amazing. Where will they go?"

"I'm not sure. Let's follow one!"

When a chick leaves its nest and flies away, we say that it has fledged.

"The chick has found Ava and Bella. But look, the dad is stealing one of Bella's caterpillars!"

"Oh no, sorry Bella! He wants to feed his chick. It has just fledged the nest so it's very hungry!"

"Alright. Just one caterpillar, for fledging the nest. I'm hoping the rest will grow into butterflies."

Mom and dad will continue to feed the chicks until they are more confident at flying. A chick can eat as many as 100 caterpillars each day!

What a busy day! I've seen so many incredible birds and I'm so happy that the chicks finally fledged.

Why don't you get to know the birds in your area? Collect feathers, put out food, or go on a bird-spotting adventure. You'll soon make lots of new feathered friends!

HOW TO BE A
NATURE HERO
≳BIRDS≲

Aren't birds amazing? We are so lucky to share our world with such fascinating creatures. Use the tips below to protect birds, and make the world a happier and safer place for them to live. Be a real-life BIRD HERO!

- Put out a bowl of clean, fresh water, so that birds and other wildlife always have something to drink.

- Grow plants that provide food and shelter for birds, such as ivy, honeysuckle and sunflowers.

- Always dispose of your litter in the correct place, to keep birds from getting hurt.

- Put up a bird box to encourage bird neighbors to move in nearby.

To protect all animals and the world they live in, it's also important to:

- Think carefully before buying new things. Try to avoid buying plastic and buy things second-hand whenever you can.

- Treat wild spaces with kindness, pick up litter, stick to the paths, and never trample on plants or fungi.

- Grow green things wherever you can. Pack your windowsill with plants or create a vegetable patch.

Pedro   Ava   Bella